PRAISE FOR ON DIGITAL ADVOCACY

"For every outdoor lover asking, 'How can I make a difference?' Katie Boué's *On Digital Advocacy* offers a clear guide for how to make an impact. The world of advocacy is changing quickly, and throughout the book, Boué's powerful voice and expertise guide you through strategies and examples for modern activism and organizing. Whether you're an individual or an organization, learn how to create impact that matters using Boué's unique combination of storytelling and case studies that are sure to inspire. Reading this book will support you in your journey to making the world a better place, whatever your cause."
  —Caroline Gleich, professional skier and climate activist

"Boué's book comes at a critical time when the worlds of advocacy and community are colliding with individuals' online presence. I think it's a must-read for folks interested in digital advocacy. But really, it's a crucial conversation for anyone working to create a true impact between their digital profiles and neighborhood community."
  —Heather Balogh Rochfort, award-winning adventure writer

"The more time we spend online, the easier it can feel to slide into binary ways of thinking: indoors or outside, burn out or sign off, advocate or give up. In the face of all that, Boué's *On Digital Advocacy* is a refreshing invitation to breathe and get curious about the things that matter most to us. And along the way, Boué generously grants us the tools we need to make a real difference—all delivered with her trademark gusto and grace."
  —Gale Straub, author of *She Explores: Stories of Life-Changing Adventures on the Road and in the Wild*

T0002644

"I looked up Outdoor Advocacy in the dictionary. It said: Katie Boué. From being a creative force behind signature campaigns (Vote the Outdoors) to demonstrating how advocacy can be part of a lifestyle (Outdoor Advocacy Project) and more (oh, so much more!), Katie has been a beacon to me when it comes to advocacy work in and for the outdoors. And now she has it in book form, providing a how-to and why-to grounded in her depth of expertise and lived experience. But one thing that Katie deeply embodies and which I respect and admire is the growth-oriented process that is crucial to this work and that keeps our humanity centered as we fight for people and planet in ways that do not destructively consume us. Because we have enough 'doom and gloom,' we need more 'do and bloom' that activates individual action in relation to our communities so we can thrive. And Katie offers us that. So do yourself a favor and read *On Digital Advocacy: Protecting the Planet While Preserving Our Humanity. Y gracias*, Katie, for your *palabras*."

—José Gonzalez, Founder at Latino Outdoors,
Educator, Creative, Facilitator

ON DIGITAL ADVOCACY

THE TOOLKIT

KATIE BOUÉ

FULCRUM PUBLISHING

Wheat Ridge, Colorado

ISBN 978-1-68275-461-0

Printed in the United States
0 9 8 7 6 5 4 3 2 1

Book design by Kateri Kramer
Illustrations by Kateri Kramer
Cover design and art by Kateri Kramer

Unless otherwise noted, all websites cited were current as of the initial edition of this book.

Fulcrum Publishing
3970 Youngfield Street
Wheat Ridge, Colorado 80033
(800) 992-2908 • (303) 277-1623
www.fulcrumbooks.com

"The land is the real teacher. All we need as students is mindfulness."
—Robin Wall Kimmerer

INTRODUCTION
LETTER TO OUTDOORISTS

Dear Outdoorist,

I'm so glad you're here.

This workbook is an invitation to get curious. It's an opportunity to celebrate the challenge and joy of finding purpose through advocacy.

Let's set some expectations together. First, a commitment to nuance and critical thinking—these are nonnegotiable tools for advocates. Practice both, daily. You must be willing to challenge your own perceptions and get uncomfortable with some of the bad habits or philosophies you may carry.

Second, we're going to get handsy with this workbook—or at least, I hope you will. By the time you're done with it, I hope these pages are scribbled with creative musings and writing that empowers you as an advocate. This is one of the few times I'll encourage you to leave a trace, make a mark, litter these pages!

I hope this workbook will become a familiar companion—that you'll complete these pages, put them into action, then return regularly to refresh and inspire yourself. My wish for you is that you run out of space from filling each paper page with notes, thoughts, and dreams. May you finally have a real excuse to buy that new notebook, and may you use it as an extension of this workbook.

I hope your advocacy becomes so big that this little handheld collection of paper can no longer contain it. May you explode from these pages.

In solidarity,

Katie B.

HOW IT WORKS

GUIDE TO USING THIS WORKBOOK

We're putting words into action—even if that action is just writing down more words. And to keep our brains juicy, there is a buffet of different activations throughout the workbook, from real-life tasks to inspiring quotes. You'll find prompts you gravitate toward and others you that make you uncomfortable—lean into them all.

Here's a quick breakdown of the different types of activations you'll find and what to expect:

JOURNAL PROMPT: These prompts are too big for the bounds of this workbook—take them to your journal or notebook of choice. Incorporate them into your current journaling rituals, or take this as an opportunity to start using one of those dozens of un-used notebooks you've been collecting over the years.

CREATIVE DUMP: Just let it all out. It's a brain-storm moment. This is one of the first places where the pages of this workbook may not suffice for holding the magnitudes of thought you're about to spill. Grab that notebook. Fill it. If I ask you to set a timer, I encourage you to keep on writing after the alarm goes off.

CASE STUDY: We'll visit real-world scenarios and historical events that have shaped advocacy and provided frameworks for what works.

ACTIVITY: Once again we're reaching beyond the bounds of this workbook, but this time we're not just hopping onto another page—we're taking things IRL.

QUOTE: Self-explanatory—because sometimes, other folks just said it better. These won't be labeled, and there's no action item for you besides: enjoy. If something resonates, jot it down on a Post-it and stick it on your bathroom mirror.

BONUS SECTIONS: From graphics to random sidebars, you'll find activations and asides throughout the workbook that were designed to keep your creativity flowing. Things might get weird; just roll with it.

ON PERMISSION

What does it mean to be an outdoor advocate? What does advocacy look like when it's put into practice? Who are we, as advocates? I offer no answers, just questions to ponder. There is no right answer, no perfect answer, no response that will qualify you to be classified as an advocate.

Advocacy is about doing your best, when you can, with what you've got. That's all you can ask for from yourself—so it's only fair to set your expectations accordingly. Be reasonable, stay humble, take your activism one step at a time. You owe it to yourself.

Permission Slip: Fill-in-the-blanks/sign your name here. P.S. There's another in the back for you to tear out and tape on your wall.

I GIVE MYSELF,_____, PERMISSION NOT TO CARRY THE BURDEN OF SAVING MOTHER EARTH WITH MY OWN TWO HANDS. I GIVE MYSELF PERMISSION TO APPROACH ADVOCACY WITH CURIOSITY AND WITHOUT GUILT/SHAME.

ADVOCACY NEEDS ACTION, REST, RECIPROCITY, ACCOUNTABILITY, CREATIVITY, COMMUNITY, AND A SPIRIT OF LEARNING. I, _____ ,WILL BE IN SERVICE TO THE OUTDOORS WHILE EMBODYING THE ABOVE.

I BELIEVE THAT OUTDOORISTS HAVE A RESPONSIBILITY TO PROTECT THE PLANET AND EACH OTHER—AND I AM COMMITTED TO BEING PART OF THE MOVEMENT TO DO GOOD FOR THE OUTDOORS.

SIGNED: _____

DATE:
_____

CREATIVE DUMP: What is advocacy to you? Get a blank piece of paper, and write the word "ADVOCACY" at the top. Then, set a timer for two minutes and list whatever verbs, adjectives, words, memories, and feelings come to mind when you think about what an advocate does.

ACCORDING TO THE MERRIAM-WEBSTER DICTIONARY, "ADVOCACY" (NOUN) IS: "THE ACT OR PROCESS OF SUPPORTING A CAUSE OR PROPOSAL."

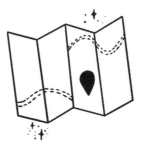

ON ADVENTURE

Advocacy requires connection, and when it comes to the outdoors, the best way to build that connection is by getting out there. When we put our boots on the ground, breathe fresh air through our lungs, witness a place for the first time with our senses—it changes us in irreversible ways.

The simple act of going to a place nearly guarantees that we will leave affected by it. Experiences in the outdoors are a natural catalyst for creating advocates. Every corner of this earth is a sight to be moved by; every experience outdoors is a moment to deepen our inherent belief that we are responsible to care and advocate for this planet. Our sense of responsibility to public lands comes through being in relationship with these places.

"IF YOU DON'T KNOW WHERE YOU ARE GOING,
EVERY ROAD WILL TAKE YOU THERE."
—LEWIS CARROLL

JOURNAL PROMPT: How has travel shaped who you are? As an advocate? As a human being? Whether visiting a local park every weekend to gather with family or going on your first camping trip, we all have one of *those* moments that deeply connected us to the outdoors. Revisit yours, dive back into the memory, write it out, describe the place, the landscape, the people you were with. Set a timer for ten minutes, and let loose on your page. Write rambling paragraphs, or jot down bulleted lists with bits of memory.

"LOOK FOR CHANCES TO TAKE THE LESS-TRAVELED ROADS. THERE ARE NO WRONG TURNS."
—SUSAN MAGSAMEN

BISON ON ANTELOPE ISLAND STATE PARK

ON BECOMING AN ADVOCATE
FOR THE OUTDOORS

What does it mean to become an advocate for the outdoors? The only prerequisite is caring about the world around you and wanting to do something about it. There's no governing body to welcome you to advocacy, no club membership, no quizzes, no playbook, and no one to keep score. (And if you encounter any of the above, run.)

BECOMING AN ADVOCATE IS A DECISION YOU MAKE.
BECOMING AN ADVOCATE IS A PERSONAL COMMITMENT.
BECOMING AN ADVOCATE IS A LIFESTYLE CHOICE.
BECOMING AN ADVOCATE IS A SPIRITUAL AWAKENING.
BECOMING AN ADVOCATE IS YOUR OWN JOURNEY.

As with many choices in life, becoming an advocate usually has a specific catalyst. Ideally, it's a powerful, proactive moment rooted in positive experience with the outdoors. Often, though, we encounter the pressing decision to be or not to be an advocate in a moment of reaction. Whether hearing about potential development looming over a local outdoor spot, or reading about faraway federal public lands losing protections, we all know the feeling of dread upon learning our beloved natural spaces are under threat—and how quickly that can press us into doing something about it.

No matter the moment that sparked you into realizing it's your duty as an outdoorist to play an active role as an advocate, our individual experiences bring us all to the same table to collaborate on solutions.

CASE STUDY: What can happen when a group of outdoorists finds their beloved spaces in peril? With the right combination of local mobilization, grassroots advocacy, and direct action, we can make an impact on the outcome of the places we cherish. Let's look at Boat Rock in Georgia. I've climbed there before and can attest: it's a southeastern bouldering gem. Here's an excerpt from the Southeastern Climbers Coalition website:

"In the late 1990's access to Boat Rock was threatened by an encroaching subdivision development. Local climbers, along with SCC, jumped into action to save this beloved boulder field. In 2005, SCC worked with the developer to purchase 7.8 acres, with another 4.5 acres donated by a climber, and a lease was secured on the Wood Hill sector in 2007.

"Boat Rock is not only known for its unique granite boulders, but also as SCC's first purchase and major acquisition project. Iconic photos of construction workers blowing up boulders while climbers scale rocks in the forefront have become a battlecry image for SCC, reminding us that access is not permanent, easy or cheap" (source: https://www.seclimbers. org/project/boat-rock/).

JOURNAL PROMPT: Have your beloved outdoors ever been under threat? Whether watching development encroach on a community bouldering spot or fighting on a national level to protect places like Bears Ears, galvanizing for landscapes in crisis is part of the outdoor identity. Reflect on a place you've watched become endangered, and spend five to ten minutes writing about the experience. What was the threat? How did the community act to resist? What was the ultimate outcome? What can you learn from how this situation played out? Has it been resolved, or is it ongoing?

PS: DID YOU END UP WRITING SOMETHING YOU'RE PARTICULARLY PROUD OF? CONSIDER ADAPTING IT INTO AN OP-ED FOR A LOCAL PUBLICATION. TAKE YOUR BLURB, SPRUCE IT UP WITH AN INTRODUCTORY PARAGRAPH TEEING UP THE ISSUE, ADD A CALL-TO-ACTION AT THE END, AND SUBMIT IT. YOUR VOICE MATTERS, AND YOUR NEIGHBORS WANT TO HEAR WHAT YOU HAVE TO SAY.

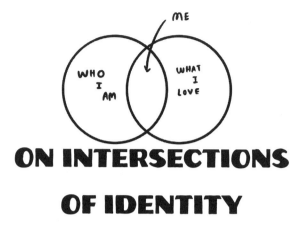

ON INTERSECTIONS

OF IDENTITY

Who we are informs how we advocate—and let's be honest, "who we are" is complicated, and so is our advocacy.

The term "intersectionality" was first conceptualized by scholar Kimberlé Crenshaw in 1989 to describe the crossover and overlapping of identities like race, class, and gender. If you Google it, the internet will tell you:"Intersectionality is an analytical framework for understanding how aspects of a person's social and political identities combine to create different modes of discrimination and privilege. Intersectionality identifies multiple factors of advantage and disadvantage" (source: https://en.wikipedia.org/wiki/Intersectionality#cite_note-Runyan-1).

GRAPHIC ACTIVITY: Who are you? I'll keep asking that question until the end of time—because the beauty and frustration is: the answer will always be in flux. Many elements of who we are as humans are static, like where we were born, but many are constantly shifting, like our favored outdoor pursuit or even where we live.

Always be answering the question of who you are, and always be asking.

Take a look at the example identity cloud, then spend five minutes filling out the blank template (or copy it into your journal).

ON THE TWO TYPES
OF ADVOCACY

GRAPHIC ACTIVITY: A fill-in-the-blank brain-storm exercise. How do you practice real-world advocacy, how do you practice digital advocacy? (How do you vs. how do you want to!)

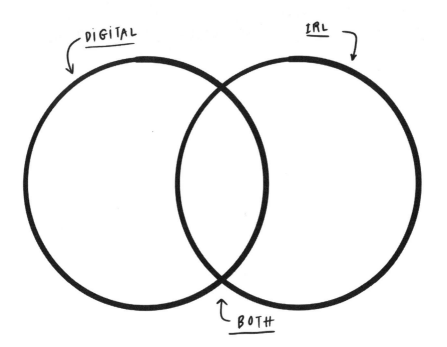

DIGITAL

IRL

BOTH

there opportunities to create better balance or shift your energies? Has the way you're practicing advocacy been working—and by that, I mean: Do you feel good in your mind, body, and soul about the ways you advocate right now? What feels good, and how can you lean deeper into it? What isn't working, and how can you address that? Set a ten-minute timer, and go.

ACCORDING TO THE UNIVERSITY OF KANSAS, "DIGITAL ADVOCACY IS THE USE OF DIGITAL TECHNOLOGY TO CONTACT, INFORM, AND MOBILIZE A GROUP OF CONCERNED PEOPLE AROUND AN ISSUE OR CAUSE" (SOURCE: HTTPS://CTB.KU.EDU/EN/TABLE-OF-CONTENTS/ADVOCACY/DIRECT-ACTION/ELECTRONIC-ADVOCACY/MAIN).

ON OUTDOORISTS

Who are you?

What do you care about?

What do you bring to the table?

How can you contribute to advocacy?

Big questions, eh? I've been asking myself these questions for more than a decade, and in 2018 I developed a worksheet that I brought to advocacy events to guide folks through the process of figuring out our identities as outdoorists—and how we can put ourselves to good use for the causes we care about.

Let's revisit that worksheet and walk through it together.

First: Who are you?

But who are you, really? This is twofold. Grab a pen, set a timer for three minutes, and fill in this next section:

We're complicated creatures with layers of complications, but we can begin to understand ourselves better when we figure out what brings us joy and what we're good at. It provides a basic framework for how we can move through the world around us as advocates. When we set ourselves up for success, we are investing in the success of the movements we seek to contribute to.

Sometimes in the various nooks and crannies of our nuanced identities, we fail to see how the different elements of who we are can intersect with each other. An avid sport climber with an accounting day job may not think the two are connected—but consider this: perhaps your local climbing coalition needs support with bookkeeping.

Are you a graphic designer who loves trout? Your art can help fuel conservation campaigns.

Are you a cyclist who owns a business in town? Offering space for convening and events is invaluable to local organizers.

Just a happy camper with a knack for baking? Drop off a dozen cupcakes during a volunteer event.

The ways we can show up as advocates are as creative and abundant as we are. When we all show up to the table offering our unique skill sets, we create an ecosystem of action that cultivates sustainable communities and causes. These contributions don't have to be grand—and small, personal acts are the best way to get started in practicing advocacy as a lifestyle.

Let's start small and identify three small actions you can commit to this week. Set yourself up for success—choose doable tasks. Examples include:

- Signing up for a trail day or local advocacy event
- Emailing an organization to learn more about volunteering
- Finding an org to donate this week's latte money to
- Researching your employer's paid volunteer time policy

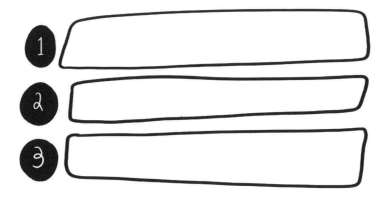

Take a look at your three options—which action speaks to you most?

Highlight or star it, and let's dive deeper into building a plan to put this idea into motion. What steps do you need to take to complete this task? Start from the bottom: What is our ultimate goal here? Then we'll work backward to fill in the steps needed to turn this advocacy intention into

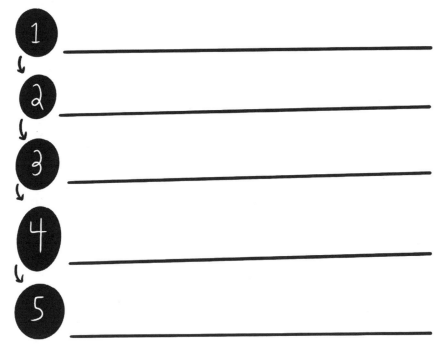

Feels good to have a plan, doesn't it? Studies show that you are more likely to complete your goals if you write them down, so you've just set yourself up to follow through. Now that you've got your goal teed up, the final step is figuring out how you can support someone else's advocacy too.

ACTIVITY: Pay attention to what your friends, family, and colleagues care about. Listen and observe—how are the people around you activating around the issues they care about? How can you support them? Offer your time to help review or edit, join them at an event for their organization of choice, help spread the word about something they're working on. Making our own individual contributions to advocacy feels good, but participating in advocacy as an act of community feels great.

ACCORDING TO A STUDY IN THE NATIONAL LIBRARY OF MEDICINE, PEOPLE WHO MAKE A REGULAR HABIT OUT OF PRACTICING KINDNESS SEE A 23 PERCENT REDUCTION IN CORTISOL, AKA THE HORMONE AT THE ROOT OF STRESS. BEING KIND AND DOING THINGS FOR OTHERS IS GOOD FOR YOU (SOURCE: HTTPS://PUBMED. NCBI.NLM.NIH.GOV/9737736/).

ON THE ROAD

To be an outdoorist is to dream of a road trip. It's just what we do. When we're not out there, experiencing nature, we're daydreaming about it. Dropping curious pins on Google Maps, collaging vision boards for faraway destinations, looking up trailhead maps for places we've never been to.

Our curiosity about getting out there is a driving force for outdoorists, and one we can use to fuel our work as advocates. Being on the road, whether in a van for a year or in a sedan for the afternoon, changes us and makes us who we are. Being on the road puts us on the path to ourselves—and that road always ends up pointing toward advocacy.

 GRAPHIC ACTIVITY: Two options: keep tabs on all the places you've been and love the most, or map out your fantasy road trip. Return to this map and keep filling it out, marking it up, and collecting outdoorist memories.

JOURNAL PROMPT: We've visited many places and memories already, but it's time to home in on just one. Without thinking, jot down your answer: What is the most impactful outdoor experience you've ever had?

YOUR ANSWER:

ACTIVITY: Write a love letter to the outdoors, specically addressed to the scene of your answer to the journal prompt above. If it's possible and feels right, grab a stamp and actually send it. An anonymous love letter, mailed to the visitor center for another steward of that place to open and enjoy.

Checklist: Consider these ideas for advocacy in action on your next road trip:

- ☐ PICK UP TRASH AROUND YOUR CAMPSITE.
- ☐ ADD IN A STOP TO THE LOCAL CONSERVANCY OR VISITOR CENTER OFFICE TO LEARN ABOUT THE AREA'S HISTORY AND HERITAGE.
- ☐ MAKE A MONETARY DONATION TO AN INDIGENOUS OR PUBLIC LANDS ORGANIZATION.
- ☐ SPEND YOUR MONEY ON LOCALLY OWNED BUSINESSES.
- ☐ LOOK UP SUPPLY NEEDS FOR LOCAL ORGANIZERS AND BRING THEM.
- ☐ DRIVE SLOWLY TO PROTECT WILDLIFE.
- ☐ OFFER LEFTOVER CAMP SUPPLIES TO YOUR NEIGHBORS BEFORE PACKING UP.

ON LOOKING AHEAD

When we're on the road or adventuring outdoors, it's hard to be anywhere but present—and that's a good thing. Time spent basking in exactly where we are, savoring every morsel of a moment, etching nature into our memories, is time well spent. Between these instances of utter presence, we ought to spend our time looking ahead in preparation for the next.

Learning to be proactive instead of reactive is a process fundamental to creating sustainability within movements. In the outdoor space, fast-changing politics and contested public lands issues mean reactivity is inherent—but in becoming well-versed in planning ahead, we set ourselves up to be able to react more nimbly when necessary.

Take a look at your year; admire the next twelve months of possibility. If you have plans, trips, volunteer ambitions—add them to this calendar. Fill in the blanks, and see what is left. Let the intersections of your birthday, vacations, family holidays, and outdoor plans take up space together. Examine where you have time, and how you might want to spend it for good. Reflect on where time is stretched thin, and plan now for how you'll keep hustle and rest balanced. Take note of the outdoor dates that excite you, and look up how you might get involved from an advocacy angle.

NOTE FOR READERS: MANY OF THESE DATES SHIFT EACH YEAR; A QUICK ONLINE SEARCH WILL LET YOU KNOW WHEN THIS YEAR'S CELEBRATIONS ARE HAPPENING!

FIRST DAY HIKES – JANUARY 1
DAY OF SERVICE – THIRD MONDAY OF JANUARY (MARTIN LUTHER KING, JR. DAY)

BLACK CLIMATE WEEK

LATINO ADVOCACY WEEK
VERNAL EQUINOX (START OF SPRING)

EARTH DAY – APRIL 22
NATIONAL PARK WEEK
NATIONAL JUNIOR RANGER DAY
NATIONAL VOLUNTEER WEEK – THIRD WEEK OF APRIL
NATIONAL ARBOR DAY – LAST FRIDAY IN APRIL
CELEBRATE TRAILS DAY – FOURTH SATURDAY IN APRIL

WILDFIRE PREPAREDNESS MONTH
WILDFLOWER WEEK – FIRST FULL WEEK OF MAY
WORLD MIGRATORY BIRD DAY – SECOND SATURDAY IN MAY
KIDS TO PARKS DAY – THIRD SATURDAY IN MAY

JUNE

GREAT OUTDOORS MONTH
NATIONAL TRAILS DAY - FIRST SATURDAY IN JUNE
NATIONAL FISHING AND BOATING WEEK - FIRST FULL WEEK
IN JUNE
NATIONAL GET OUTDOORS DAY - SECOND SATURDAY IN JUNE
GREAT AMERICAN CAMPOUT - FOURTH SATURDAY IN JUNE
SUMMER SOLSTICE (START OF SUMMER)

JULY

NATIONAL PARKS AND RECREATION MONTH
LATINO CONSERVATION WEEK

AUGUST

SMOKEY BEAR'S BIRTHDAY - AUGUST 9
NATIONAL PARK SERVICE BIRTHDAY - AUGUST 25

SEPTEMBER

NATIONAL WILDLIFE DAY - SEPTEMBER 4
NATIONAL PUBLIC LANDS DAY - FOURTH SATURDAY IN SEP-
TEMBER
AUTUMNAL EQUINOX (START OF FALL)

OCTOBER

INDIGENOUS PEOPLE'S DAY - OCTOBER 10
NATIONAL WILDLIFE REFUGE WEEK - SECOND FULL WEEK OF
OCTOBER
URBAN WILDLIFE CONSERVATION DAY - SECOND SATURDAY OF
OCTOBER

NOVEMBER

NATIVE AMERICAN HERITAGE MONTH
NATIONAL TAKE A HIKE DAY - NOVEMBER 17
NATIVE AMERICAN HERITAGE DAY - FOURTH FRIDAY OF NOVEMBER
GREEN FRIDAY/#OPTOUTSIDE DAY - FOURTH FRIDAY OF NOVEMBER

DECEMBER

WINTER SOLSTICE (START OF WINTER)

OTHER DAYS to REMEMBER

_____

_____

_____

_____

_____

_____

_____

_____

_____

_____

ON VOTING

The highest of all outdoor advocate duties: our civic responsibility to vote. I wish I never had to hear the words "this is the most important election of our lifetime" ever again, but the reality is, every modern election has been critical and will continue to be. Voting is frustrating—infuriating, even—but it's important. Not everyone has access to voting rights, and those of us who do are indebted to those who cannot cast their own ballots.

Voting puts politicians into office, and those politicians make choices. The president you elect gets to use the Antiquities Act to designate monuments; your state and local officials will be the ones making decisions about parks and trails in your neighborhoods. State legislatures will directly shape the fate of places like the Great Salt Lake. Our ballots help decide the hands that will pen our futures.

When we vote, we cast our opinions on our environment, neighborhoods, waterways, air, and the entire planet. Vote with your neighbors in mind. Vote the outdoors.

"VOTING IS THE EXPRESSION OF OUR COMMITMENT TO OURSELVES, ONE ANOTHER, THIS COUNTRY, AND THIS WORLD."
—SUSAN SALZBERG

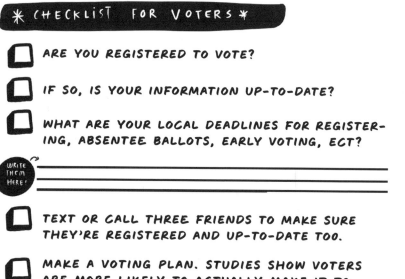

✳ CHECKLIST FOR VOTERS ✳

☐ ARE YOU REGISTERED TO VOTE?

☐ IF SO, IS YOUR INFORMATION UP-TO-DATE?

☐ WHAT ARE YOUR LOCAL DEADLINES FOR REGISTER-ING, ABSENTEE BALLOTS, EARLY VOTING, ECT?

(WRITE THEM HERE!)
_____
_____
_____

☐ TEXT OR CALL THREE FRIENDS TO MAKE SURE THEY'RE REGISTERED AND UP-TO-DATE TOO.

☐ MAKE A VOTING PLAN. STUDIES SHOW VOTERS ARE MORE LIKELY TO ACTUALLY MAKE IT TO THE POLLS WHEN THEY HAVE A PLAN. HOW ARE YOU VOTING? WHEN? WRITE IT DOWN ON THE NEXT PAGE.
(SOURCE: HTTPS://SCHOLAR.HARVARD.EDU/FILES/TODD_RODGERS/FILES/ DO_YOU_HAVEA_VOTING_PLAN_0.PDF

☐ RESEARCH, RESEARCH, RESEARCH. GET TO KNOW THE CANDIDATES, BALLOT ISSUES, AND KEY RACES. SEEK VOTER GUIDES FROM ORGANI-ZATIONS AND LOCAL LEADERS YOU TRUST.

☐ FIGURE OUT HOW TO CAST YOUR BALLOT. MANY STATES HAVE VOTE-BY-MAIL AND EARLY VOTING OPTIONS—GET IT DONE AS EARLY AS YOU CAN. IF YOU PLAN TO HEAD OUT ON ELECTION DAY, BE SURE TO LOOK UP YOUR POLLING PLACE AND DOUBLE-CHECK ANY NECESSARY ID OR LOCAL REQUIREMENTS

☐ FOLLOW UP TO ENSURE YOUR VOTE IS COUNTED. DID YOU KNOW MOST STATES EMPOWER YOU TO CHECK THE STATUS OF YOUR BALLOT ONLINE? MANY ARE REJECTED DUE TO EASILY FIXED IS-SUES LIKE MISSING SIGNATURES. SO MAKE SURE YOU CHECK AND RECONCILE YOUR BALLOT IF NEEDED.
(TRACK YOUR BALLOT HERE: HTTPS://WWW.VOTE.ORG/BALLOT-TRACK-ER-TOOLS/).

MY VOTING PLAN!

_____

_____

_____

_____

_____

_____

_____

_____

_____

_____

_____

_____

_____

_____

_____

_____

_____

_____

_____

_____

_____

ON ORGANIZING

"TRYING TO MAKE THINGS BETTER THROUGH ORGANIZING AND SOCIAL CHANGE WAS ANOTHER WAY FOR ME TO BELIEVE IN THE POTENTIAL OF OUR SPECIES RATHER THAN TO ACCEPT AND BE COMPLICIT IN THE DESTRUCTION WE REAP."
—ADRIENNE MAREE BROWN

checklist ↗ WHAT to DO to GET INFORMED and TAKE ACTION WHEN an ISSUE ⋛POPS⋚ UP that YOU ARE INTERESTED IN.

☐ STEP UNO! BECOME A STUDENT. LEARN EVERYTHING YOU CAN ABOUT THE ISSUE. THE BEST INFORMATION COMES FROM LOCAL EXPERTS, BUT A QUICK GOOGLE SEARCH CAN YIELD EXCELLENT LEADS ON RESOURCES TOO. ABSORB EVERYTHING YOU CAN ABOUT THE ISSUE AND TAKE NOTES.

☐ STEP DOS! FIGURE OUT KEY TALKING POINTS. DISTILLED INTO THREE TO FIVE SENTENCES: WHAT IS THE PROBLEM? WHY DOES IT MATTER? AND WHAT IS THE PROPOSED SOLUTION? HAVING CONCISE MESSAGING HELPS YOU COMMUNICATE THE TOPIC AND HELPS OTHERS MORE EASILY UNDERSTAND WHAT'S GOING ON.

WHAT IS THE PROBLEM? _____

_____

WHY DOES IT MATTER? _____

_____

WHAT IS THE PROPOSED SOLUTION? _____

_____

☐ **STEP TRES!** ZERO IN ON DECISION MAKERS WHO ARE THE MAIN STAKEHOLDERS INVOLVED WITH THE ISSUE, AND HOW YOU CAN CONTACT THEM. IT COULD BE ANYONE FROM THE PRESIDENT TO A PRIVATE LANDOWNER.

☐ **STEP QUATRO!** IDENTIFY THE CALL TO ACTION. THIS HAS LIKELY ALREADY BEEN DONE FOR YOU. WHAT IS THE TO-DO HERE? POTENTIAL CALLS TO ACTION INCLUDE SIGNING A PETITION, CONTACTING LAWMAKERS, ATTENDING AN EVENT, WRITING A PUBLIC COMMENT, ETC.

☐ **STEP CINCO!** FOLLOW THROUGH AND FOLLOW UP. PUT THE CALL TO ACTION IN MOTION. RECRUIT YOUR COMMUNITY TO JOIN YOU. AFTERWARD, WRAP IT ALL UP WITH A "THANK YOU"—WHETHER IT'S YOUR LAWMAKERS, LOCAL ORGANIZERS, OR EVEN ON SOCIAL MEDIA.

ON HOW TO BUILD A SOCIAL MEDIA TOOLKIT

Follow the guidelines below to create your own social media toolkit.

Start by putting logo(s) in the header.

LOGO(S) IN THE HEADER

CAMPAIGN TITLE

NAME OF THE ORANNIZING ENTITIES

MONTH, YEAR

Introduction to the campaign, who is organizing it, why it's happening—overall this is the spot to dump the main bulk of messaging about what you're doing and why the reader should lend their time and energy to be part of it. Include your mission, identify the problem/solutions, name key stakeholders, and include what the "ask" is.
[Got a Graphic/Logo specific to this campaign? Insert here!]

HOW TO GET INVOLVED:

This should be the number-one action if they only do one thing for this campaign (so, "take the pledge" or "send your senator the letter").
Invite them to share their action online. This is usually where I'd say: download the graphics here!

Offer ideas for social posts; be sure to mention #YourHashtag.
Stay tuned. This is a great place to drop retention links like signing up for a newsletter to keep updated.

SUGGESTED MESSAGING:

Here is where you'll have about three to five suggestions for social media posts.

I like to include two shorter and one longer option. The caption would look something like this, with a call to action to do something: [and a link] #WithAHashtag

Clickable thumbnails of any additional graphics:

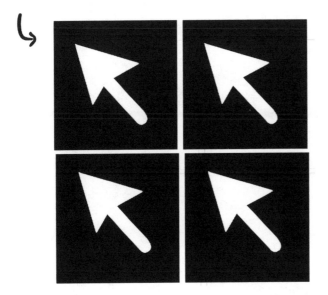

End it with contact information; e.g., someone's e-mail address.

ON THE ADVOCACY RETENTION CYCLE

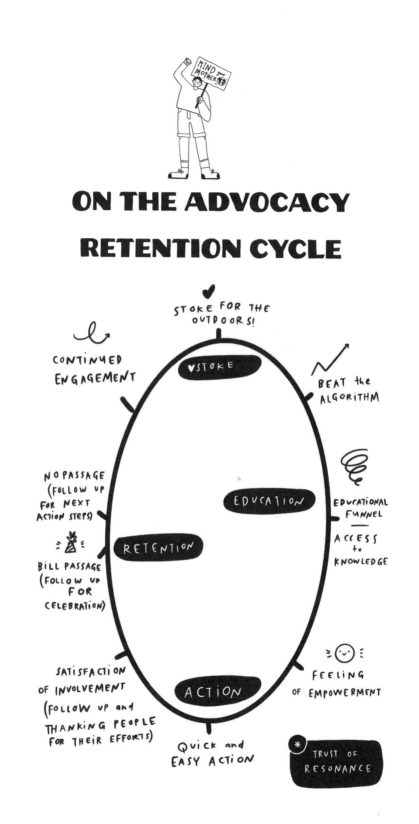

JOURNAL PROMPT: Let's examine where the cycle fails. The final step, retention, is where many advocacy moments reach an abrupt halt. How can we better follow through with campaigns and leave our community feeling more energized for a return? Think about an advocacy issue you're active on right now––or start making one up.

Set a timer for five minutes (this will be a twenty-five-minute total activity). Starting with **Stoke**, create a header at the top of the page, then spend five minutes brain dumping about the stoke element behind your campaign. Why does this matter? Who cares? How does that community like to rally?

Next, **Education**: What kind of information do people need in order to fully understand the topic? What types of resources and data are available? Who is currently working on this issue?

Third, **Action**: The climax. What are we going to do about this? Is it a formal comment period, in-person event, online petition, fundraiser, art installation?

Last, **Retention**: How can we keep the momentum going from this moment? Is there a final step needed to complete this activation? Who can we send gratitude to?

Spend your final five minutes focused on the idea of retention. If you're using a real-world scenario, critically examine the success rate of follow-through—were you even able to measure it? How can we more thoughtfully strategize to collect and continually activate our community contacts after a big moment of Action?

CASE STUDY: Can a nationally beloved destination garner enough attention to protect a parcel of land from oil and gas development? Spoiler alert: Yes. In the summer of 2020, we learned that more than 114,000 acres of land in Utah were being proposed for an oil and gas leasing sale by the Bureau of Land Management. More than 80,000 of those acres were located around Moab, and this lease sale could have heavily impacted recreation and sacred land. Our team at Outdoor Advocacy Project partnered with Public Land Solutions to create a social media campaign to gather signatures for a petition by outdoor users—to support their larger movement of local Moab city officials, businesses, and other concerned citizens.

Our initial goal was 5,000 signatures—but I was hoping that the universal lore of Moab's desert landscapes could reach far beyond our statewide community contingencies.

And it did.

By the end of the campaign, we had gathered more than 36,000 signatures, and we delivered the petition to Department of Interior secretary David Bernhardt and Utah governor Gary Herbert. Public Land Solutions also organized statements from local officials and collective sign-on letters from businesses to create a powerful ecosystem of concerned stakeholders.

In August 2020, we received word that the Bureau of Land Management had officially canceled the planned auction.

ON INFLUENCE

In this age of connectivity and digital identities, we must be savvy about how to be a responsible advocate through social media. I'm not suggesting that you become an influencer, but if you do. . . . This is not a how-to on how to get 10K followers, it's a framework for people with influential digital spaces to use them for good.

And by "people with influential digital spaces," I mean you.
We must examine and put into critical reflection the idea that everything we post on social media is, in essence, a performance. And that's okay—it allows us to see the limitations and honest levels of impact provided by posting online. Guide folks through the incredibly uncomfortable idea that social media is all a curated performance, give permission for that to be okay, and turn it into a powerful moment of clarity.

 ACTIVITY: Clean up your feed! We clean out the cuboard, our closets, our desks—tidying up our spaces is an integral part of keeping a healthy personal ecosystem. That philosophy applies to the digital space too.

Set a timer for ten minutes. Open up your social media platform of choice, and click your "following" list. Scroll through it, and without hesitation, slam the unfollow button whenever you reach a name on that list that does not spark joy. If it's someone you can't unfollow, like a family member or work relation, just mute them. Repeat for each of your social media platforms. Do not follow people who make you feel bad. Enduring self-inflicted suffering on your social media is never worth it.

ON BURNOUT

If you do not give yourself permission to take the break you need, you will start to suffer. And suffering is helpful to no one.

"THE CURE FOR DEPRESSION IS ACTION. EVERY ONE OF US HAS TO STEP UP AND DO WHAT YOU CAN, ACCORDING TO WHAT RESOURCES YOU HAVE."
—YVON CHOUINARD

Purpose and action drive a fulfilled life. But sometimes, life just sucks. Period. When you have nothing left to give, no amount of forcing yourself to show up and advocate is going to cure the blues. Sometimes, you just need rest. Take it.

Action is the cure for apathy, but when tired advocates require rest, our inaction does not equate to becoming apathetic. Rest is worthy. Rest is necessary. Rest enables action.

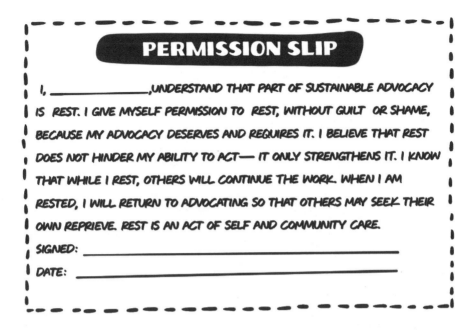

PERMISSION SLIP

I, _____, UNDERSTAND THAT PART OF SUSTAINABLE ADVOCACY IS REST. I GIVE MYSELF PERMISSION TO REST, WITHOUT GUILT OR SHAME, BECAUSE MY ADVOCACY DESERVES AND REQUIRES IT. I BELIEVE THAT REST DOES NOT HINDER MY ABILITY TO ACT— IT ONLY STRENGTHENS IT. I KNOW THAT WHILE I REST, OTHERS WILL CONTINUE THE WORK. WHEN I AM RESTED, I WILL RETURN TO ADVOCATING SO THAT OTHERS MAY SEEK THEIR OWN REPRIEVE. REST IS AN ACT OF SELF AND COMMUNITY CARE.

SIGNED: _____

DATE: _____

LOOKING FOR FURTHER READING ON BURNOUT? CHECK OUT BURNOUT: THE SECRET TO UNLOCKING THE STRESS CYCLE BY EMILY NAGOSKI, PHD AND AMELIA NAGOSKI, DMA

MENTAL-HEALTH
CHECKPOINT

Friend, you've reached a mental-health checkpoint. We've been going hard, diving in, exploring our advocacy, and challenging our perspectives—and now it's time to pause for a moment.

Inhale, exhale.

Go get a glass of water.

Drink it, then fill it back up.

Now set a timer for twenty minutes and take a break with this page. Color it in, trace your pen over the outlines, add your own embellishments—whatever feels good to you. Maybe you don't want to doodle at all but instead want to spend these twenty minutes breathing deep with your eyes closed. That's cool too.

Good advocacy requires sustainable stewards, and stewards require rest.

Take this twenty-minute break.

You deserve it.

A MOMENT OF
DIGITAL HYGIENE

ACTIVITY: Audit your digital presence. Digital privacy is one of the most critical elements of protecting yourself online—and once you lose privacy on the internet, it's hard to regain it.

Google yourself. Dig deep in the search results and see what identifying information of yours is publicly available.

Things to look out for: addresses via public records, personal contact information like your phone number or email, and identifying information about any family members.

There are services that will remove these search results to bolster your privacy, but the best solution here is prevention. Be wary of where you share your address, or better yet, use a PO box. Just because people can find you online doesn't mean you want them having access to you in real life.

ACTIVITY: Good digital hygiene isn't all about the spooky practice of protecting your privacy—it can also be an exercise in creative identity communication. Who are you, and how do want to communicate yourself to the world?

You know that classic concept of dressing for the job you want, not the one you have? Let's apply that to the digital space—how you dress your online presence affects how you present yourself to the infinite world wide web.

Let's start with your main social media channels: Instagram, Twitter, Facebook, TikTok—whatever platforms you use. Take a peek at your bio—does it declare your advocacy intentions? Does it make connections to the places and issues you're most passionate about? How about your avatar? If you're a climber who focuses your advocacy on desert landscapes, consider updating your profile image to match.

Less sexy: a quick audit of your LinkedIn account and résumé will directly set you up for the advocacy position you want to be in. Don't have experience working specifically in advocacy roles? List your extracurriculars like organization memberships, community involvement, etc. Use the "About" section to share your nonemployment-related advocacy passions and goals.

"FINDING BEAUTY IN A BROKEN WORLD IS CREATING BEAUTY IN
THE WORLD WE FIND."
—TERRY TEMPEST WILLIAMS

ON THE END

You may not realize it, but you've been gardening. Throughout this workbook, you've been tilling your own soil, uprooting yourself, grounding yourself, and planting little seeds. These tiny nuggets are meant to keep nourishing you long after this workbook is closed. Set yourself up for sustainable advocacy for the rest of the year, for the rest of your life.

You might remember these from the book, but these ideas can't be repeated enough:
- Stop taking yourself so seriously all the time. Be weird, make art.
- Keep it human.
- Be wary of experts.
- You have two hands to hold two different things at the same time. Use that skill often.
- Keep it sustainable—not just for the planet, but for yourself.
- You can't be everything all the time.
- Examine the sense of urgency, and remember that it's likely not that urgent.
- Related: You don't have to respond right away.
- You actually just don't need to be online, at all.

We all share a responsibility as outdoorists to protect this planet—including ourselves and our neighbors—but that duty doesn't have to be a downer. Advocacy is an invitation to expand our hopes of what the future might look like. Advocacy is an opportunity to be part of solutions. You are the solution.

"EVERYTHING DEPENDS ON OUR ABILITY TO SUSTAINABLY IN-
HABIT THIS EARTH, AND TRUE SUSTAINABILITY WILL REQUIRE US
ALL TO CHANGE OUR WAY OF THINKING ON HOW WE TAKE FROM
THE EARTH AND HOW WE GIVE BACK."
—SECRETARY DEB HAALAND

OUTDOORIST BINGO, BECAUSE WE OUGHT TO HAVE A LITTLE FUN ON THE WAY OUT!

ADDITIONAL READING

BOOKS

- *All We Can Save: Truth, Courage, and Solutions for the Climate Crisis,* edited by Ayana Elizabeth Johnson and Katharine K. Wilkinson (One World, 2020).
- *Braiding Sweetgrass: Indigenous Wisdom, Scientific Knowledge, and the Teachings of Plants*, by Robin Wall Kimmerer (Milkweed Editions, 2020).
- *Burnout: The Secret to Unlocking the Stress Cycle*, by Emily Nagoski, PhD and Amelia Nagoski, DMA (Ballantine Books, 2019).
- *Emergent Strategy*, by adrienne maree brown (AK Press, 2017).
- *The Hour of Land: A Personal Topography of America's National Parks*, by Terry Tempest Williams (Sarah Crichton Books, 2016).
- *The Intersectional Environmentalist: How to Dismantle Systems of Oppression to Protect People + Planet*, by Leah Thomas (Voracious, 2022).
- *Pleasure Activism: The Politics of Feeling Good*, by adrienne maree brown (AK Press, 2019).
- *Tools for Grassroots Activists: Best Practices for Success in the Environmental Movement*, edited by Nora Gallagher and Lisa Myers (Patagonia, 2016).

DIGITAL RESOURCES

- Outdoor Recreation Satellite Account, US and States from the Bureau of Economic Development—"Measures the economic activity as well as the sales or receipts generated by outdoor recreational activities, such as fishing and RVing. These statistics also measure each industry's production of outdoor goods and services and its contribution to US GDP. Industry breakdowns of outdoor employment and compensation are also included" (https://www.bea.gov/data/special-topics/outdoor-recreation).

- The Public Lands Curriculum from The Wilderness Society—Framed through six topic modules, this extensive educational resource was developed to tell a more "authentic and complete story of public lands" (https://www.wilderness.org/articles/article/public-lands-united-states-curriculum).
- Together Outdoors Resource Hub by the Outdoor Recreation Roundtable—A comprehensive collection of resources focused on "understanding how we can build an outdoor community where everyone belongs" (https://resourcehub.togetheroutdoors.com).

PERMISSION SLIP

I GIVE MYSELF, _____ ,PERMISSION NOT TO CARRY THE BURDEN OF SAVING MOTHER EARTH WITH MY OWN TWO HANDS. I GIVE MYSELF PERMISSION TO APPROACH ADVOCACY WITH CURIOSITY AND WITHOUT GUILT/SHAME.

ADVOCACY NEEDS ACTION, REST, RECIPROCOCITY, ACCOUNTABILITY, CREATIVITY, COMMUNITY, AND A SPIRIT OF LEARNING. I, _____ ,WILL BE IN SERVICE TO THE OUTDOORS WHILE EMBODYING THE ABOVE.

I BELIEVE THAT OUTDOORISTS HAVE A RESPONSIBILITY TO PROTECT THE PLANET AND EACH OTHER, AND I AM COMMITTED TO BEING PART OF THE MOVEMENT TO DO GOOD FOR THE OUTDOORS.

SIGNED: _____

DATE: _____